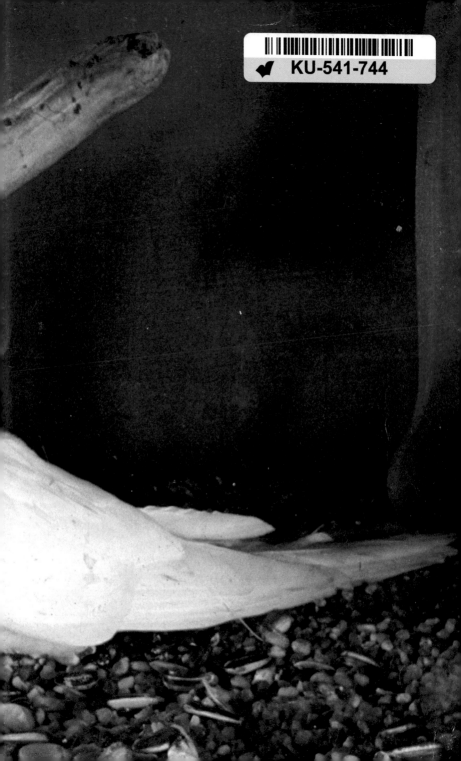

CONTENTS

Endpapers: Front endpaper by Glen S. Axelrod, left back endpaper by San Diego Zoo and right back endpaper by Fritz Prenzel.
Front Cover: Dr. Herbert R. Axelrod
Back Cover: Dr. Gerald R. Allen
Frontis: Harry V. Lacey.

Photo Credits: *Black and white photos,* Dr. Gerald R. Allen: 33, 44 (bottom); Glen S. Axelrod: 12, 17, 36, 37, 53, 63, 69, 73, 76, 84, 85; Dr. Herbert R. Axelrod: 28, 45, 47, 54, 55, 58, 59, 68 (top); Manuel Guevara: 38, 50 (at the Patterson Bird Store); John Jarret: 51; Harry V. Lacey, 5, 46; John Rammel: 32; Brian Seed: 39, 57, 62; Louise van der Meid: 16, 44 (top), 60, 68 (bottom). *Color photos,* Dr. Gerald R. Allen: 6, 15, 26, 27, 30, 66, 78, 82; Glen S. Axelrod: 18, 19, 22, 23, 71 (bottom); Dr. Herbert R. Axelrod: 79, 83; Harry V. Lacey: 66, 74, 75; P. Leysen: 90; Brian Seed: 7, 10, 14, 31, 70, 87; Vogel Park, Walsrode: 11 (top), 71 (top); Dr. Matthew M. Vriends: 11 (bottom).

Photos by Glen S. Axelrod taken with the cooperation of Rich Myles and Pets Ahoy Pet Shop of Bradley Beach, New Jersey

ISBN 0-87666-885-6

Distributed in the U.S. by T.F.H. Publications, Inc., 211 West Sylvania Avenue, PO Box 427, Neptune, NJ 07753; in England by T.F.H. (Gt. Britain) Ltd., 13 Nutley Lane, Reigate, Surrey; in Canada to the book store and library trade by Beaverbooks Ltd., 150 Lesmill Road, Don Mills, Ontario M38 2T5, Canada; in Canada to the pet trade by Rolf C. Hagen Ltd., 3225 Sartelon Street, Montreal 382, Quebec; in Southeast Asia by Y.W. Ong, 9 Lorong 36 Geylang, Singapore 14; in Australia and the South Pacific by Pet Imports Pty. Ltd., P.O. Box 149, Brookvale 2100, N.S.W. Australia; in the British Crown Colony of Hong Kong, in South Africa by Valid Agencies, P.O. Box 51901, Randburg 2125 South Africa. Published by T.F.H. Publications, Inc., Ltd.

COCKATIELS

LAURA M. TARTAK

The cockatiel is the only species of its genus, and aviculturists say that it is the connecting link between parrots and cockatoos. Shown at left is a wild bird; the albino cockatiel (below) is one of the oldest mutations.

Introduction

Of the many parrots and parrot-like birds that are available today the cockatiel appears to be the ideal pet parrot. In popularity it occupies a position between the very popular budgerigar (best known in the United States as a parakeet) and the very exotic and larger parrots (macaws, cockatoos, etc.). It is true that there are some parrots of the same size as the cockatiel and often more colorful, but such birds are not as easily available nor as well known in their habits.

An apartment dweller who does not have much space to spare and has neighbors to consider but wants to have a pet parrot can choose a cockatiel. Its cage would take up very little space; this bird does not have a raucous and irritating voice and is easy to tame.

Cockatiels are relatively inexpensive in comparison to other parrots and yet not so commonplace as budgies. They are available through bird dealers and breeders and are sold in some pet shops or even in some department stores. It will not be difficult to get a pair of cockatiels; the sexes are distinct externally. Both sexes are capable of talking although males seem to have a greater aptitude for talking than females. They whistle and imitate tunes.

These gregarious birds get along with other small species of parrots, budgerigars, finches, etc. They have a relatively long life span (about 15 to 20 years or more in captivity).

THE WILD COCKATIEL

At present the cockatiel is scientifically known as *Nymphicus hollandicus*. Modern taxonomists or systematists (qualified scientific classifiers) are not agreed as to the exact position of the cockatiel in relation to other parrots. However, it is a very distinct species and it deserves its own genus (species group). Some taxonomists and behaviorists align it with the cockatoos in a separate family (Cacatuidae) while others are of the opinion that all these birds are members of a very large parrot family (Psittacidae).

The cockatiel as its scientific name indicates was first discovered in eastern Australia (Australia was known as New Holland then). Although the bird has been cited in early books under different names and at one time incorrectly (invalid since the name given belongs legitimately to another parrot species from another continent), it received its present name in 1832, when the genus *Nymphicus* was suggested by Wagler. However, the cockatiels since the voyages of discovery of Captain Cook were not exactly unrecognized and were reported by the naturalists who were with Captain Cook during his trip to eastern Australia in 1770. They were described and published later although in a manner not acceptable to modern methods of nomenclature.

As communications and travel improved between the colonies and Great Britain, scientists collected specimens for their museums and naturalists were able to describe the habitat of the cockatiel. Through expeditions specimens were brought into England and Europe.

The cockatiel species is distributed through the Australian continent but absent in Tasmania. The systematic history (synonymy) of the cockatiel indicates that some taxonomists see differences present in populations from different areas of Australia. Nevertheless, according to most scientists these differences are not enough to justify splitting the species into subspecies.

In the wild, cockatiels (according to the great British naturalist John Gould) are more numerous in the eastern than in the western regions of Australia. His observations were made about the middle of the last century. He reported that large numbers of cockatiels (known to him as cockatoo parrakeets) cover the ground while feeding. They are found in groups, seem to prefer dead branches of trees, are capable of sustained flight and frequent areas close to streams. It is not a timid bird and, since it is good for eating, many are killed by the natives.

The wild cockatiel inhabits much of Australia, particularly the drier inlands away from the coastal regions. These birds are found near water sites such as rivers, streams and creeks and their movements are controlled by the availability of a water supply.

Cockatiels seem to favor the eastern or western parts of Australia as breeding grounds. Each year a considerable number of pairs gather in the wooded areas adjacent to rivers and streams. An etching of these cockatiels resting by

Cockatiels are universally considered to be one of the most free-breeding of all parrots. Their general breeding management is similar to that of budgerigars. Birds bred frequently in captivity over a long course of time generally produce a number of different color varieties, and the cockatiel is no exception. Three cockatiel color varieties shown here are: 1. pearled; 2. albino; 3. normal gray.

1

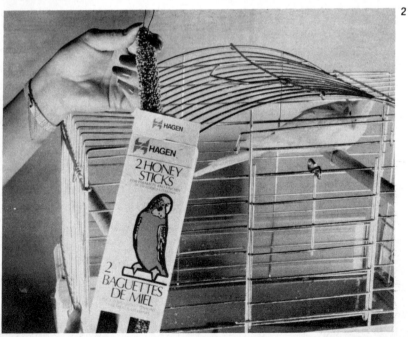

2

a creek appears in *Cassell's Book of Birds.* These birds usually prefer to make their nests in holes, hollow branches, or in a decaying stump of a dead tree; only necessity will coerce them into nesting in live trees. Wild cockatiels lay their eggs on a bed of decayed wood or on chippings that are the bottom of a scooped out saucer-shaped depression made in their nesting hole. No nesting materials are used. The eggs are white, oval-shaped and vary from four to seven according to the maturity of the birds and the time of year.

These cockatiels feed on seeds of many grasses and herbage, leaves and bark from plants, and bushes and trees that grow on the vast Australian plains. Seasonal grubs and insects are also consumed by these ground eaters.

Wild cockatiels are usually tolerant of human beings, so it is not unusual to find them in gardens and parks of built-up areas. If a cockatiel is frightened by a sudden movement it will simply fly to a nearby tree and remain there until the human disturbance passes by. Being gregarious they travel from site to site in numbers; it is rare to find a solitary wild cockatiel.

1. Millet spray may be rather expensive, but it is well worth feeding to all your cockatiels! If they have the choice of millet in a pot or millet in the spray in which it was grown, they will certainly choose the spray first! 2. Hanging a millet-compound in the cockatiel cage.

1

2

In the wild cockatiels
are found in Australia
and are widely
distributed over much
of the interior. On the
east coast they
seldom occur, only
occasionally visiting
the coast during
years with excep-
tionally low rainfall.
The white cockatiel
(1) is a domestically
bred bird; its color is
sex-linked in its man-
ner of inheritance. 2.
Wild cockatiel eating
vegetation 3. Typical
wild cockatiel habitat
in Australia.

3

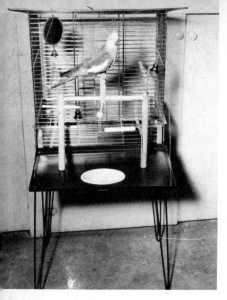

As cockatiels are birds of some 13 inches in over-all length, they will need to be housed in suitably large cages—don't crowd them into tiny finch cages. Breeding pairs can be housed in large all-wire square or round parrot cages, pens, indoor aviaries, and flighted or unflighted garden aviaries according to the space available to the breeder. *Below:* In choosing a suitable cockatiel cage, rely on your pet dealer's advice.

Housing

Cockatiels are approximately 13 inches long and should be housed in similar but larger structures than budgerigars or canaries. Wooden or all-wire parrot cages (square or round) make good homes for single pet cockatiels. Breeding pairs are often housed in large cages, pens, indoor aviaries, and flighted or unflighted garden aviaries depending upon the breeder's space availability. For exhibition purposes, large stock cages are needed for the bird's initial training. Budgerigars, finch-like species, and most cockatiels of all colors are very friendly toward one another and consequently make ideal inmates for a large or small collection of mixed aviary housing.

3

4

Gravel paper should be provided in every cage. A gravel mixture also is essential, as it is an important source of minerals. A good mixture is "red cross grit" and crushed oyster shell (both one pound) and two pounds of 'normal' gravel, which, hopefully, contains a bit of charcoal.
1. A selection of gravel paper and other bird-related accessories.
2. Preparing the paper for placement. 3. Placing the paper at the bottom of the cage. 4. Grit is being placed loosely on the bottom of the cage; more desirable would be to put it in a separate container.

Cockatiels do not fly as much or as frequently as other smaller parrot species, but nevertheless, they require a reasonable amount of flying and exercise room if they are to remain in a healthy, fit, vigorous condition.

Most breeders find that cockatiels reproduce at their greatest capacity when housed in aviaries, particularly ones with access to an outside flight. The size of the flight should be about twice the length of the sleeping quarters. If the sleeping area were 6½ feet long, then the flight should be approximately 13 feet in length. The actual size of an aviary is controlled by the amount of available space and the number of birds required by the breeder. The density of a colony population may be greater than other parakeets because cockatiels are so amenable. Breeders, though, should realize that overcrowding an aviary is undesirable if successful breeding results are to be obtained.

Cockatiels are gnawers; they quickly kill growing shrubs and any other living plants placed in their cages. Grasses of various kinds can be grown successfully on the floor of a flight to provide green food and a playground for the birds. Perches must be placed in the flight to give the birds an opportunity to gnaw. If possible, the perches should be made from branches of fruit, hazelnut, willow, alder, elm, hawthorn, sloe, or similar trees. Machine dowelling may be used if the breeder cannot obtain natural perches. Small twigs of the above mentioned trees ought to be given to cockatiels. These birds need certain amounts of green food, especially during the breeding periods. In addition, by supplying these birds with this extra gnawing material, the risk of damaging the aviary's wooden parts is reduced. The breeder needs to periodically renew all types of perching. If the perches are not firmly fixed, mating may not be successful and eggs are then clear or not fertile. Cockatiel perches should be considerably greater in diameter than those of a budgerigar or canary.

A wide range of materials can be used to build new aviaries suitable for keeping and breeding cockatiels. Various kinds of existing buildings can easily be adapted for the same purposes. The breeder must first decide whether he wants colony or single pair control breeding. It is advisable to find out from the local government if there are any regulations concerning building a garden aviary. Urban areas are usually zoned as to what types of structures can be built.

If a breeder has chosen serious color production, then the single pair method must be employed to have complete control over each breeding pair. One breeding pair to a compartment—this is the only way pedigrees may be guaranteed. Cockatiels are gregarious, but the greatest number of young are produced when pairs are separate but within sight and hearing range of other breeding pairs. A flighted (or unflighted) compartment should be at least 2½ feet in width to allow flying room for the birds.

A sleeping and feeding shelter and an outside wire flight are the important sections of an uncontrolled flighted aviary for cockatiels or for a mixed collection of birds. The sleeping quarters should be well constructed and free from dampness and drafts. Cockatiels may not require a heater during winter but freezing temperature within the shelter must be avoided.

The wire flight itself can be covered with ordinary wire mesh or with the newer welded wire mesh. Cockatiels are large birds and 3/4 or 1 inch mesh will be adequate, while a mixed collection will require 1/2 or 5/8 inch mesh. Heavy gauge wire with a coat of long-lasting non-toxic paint can also be used. This wire has a very long and useful life.

Many breeders have found that if a part of the top of the wired flight next to the sleeping quarters is covered with fiberglass or plastic sheeting, the birds can enjoy the flight during wet or snowy weather. The upper sides can also be covered with clear plastic for protection of both adult and young birds. The breeder ought to secure the floor of the

1. Regardless of how attentive you are to the nutritional needs of your pet in providing a varied diet, it makes good sense to make up for potential deficiencies by adding a good-quality vitamin/mineral supplement to the staple diet. 2. Cockatiels and other parrots are avid chewers of wood, and wood placed into their living quarters will soon be splintered. 3 and 4. The water and seed given to your cockatiel **must** be fresh and clean.

3 4

sleeping quarters against vermin. Concrete, close heavy wooden boards, and precast stone slabs may be used to protect the sleeping quarter floor, while the floor of the wire flight may be either grassed over, covered with fine gravel or sand, or grass and gravel may be combined. Possible entry of rodents can be prevented by sinking an "L" shaped strip of ½ inch (small mesh) wire netting about 8 inches into the ground completely encircling the aviary. This procedure should keep out all rats and larger mice; smaller ones can be exterminated before they mature. Patented mouse baits found at pet shops and drug stores can efficiently destroy these rodents. They are detrimental to nesting birds; they foul the water and food and often cause health hazards.

The perches in the wire flights should be decorative, but more importantly, give the birds the maximum amount of flying space. If the flight is grassed, then the portion beneath the perches ought to be cleared and filled in with sand or gravel for easy cleaning. Any type of perch can be used in the sleeping quarters as long as they are firmly fixed. They should not be placed directly above seed, grit, or water holders. This precaution applies to all bird housings.

The seed vessels ought to be good, solid utensils that will stand firmly on a shelf, table or floor. They can be made of pottery, earthenware, glass or galvanized metal. These necessary vessels should be placed in an accessible spot for both the birds and the keeper.

Older garden sheds, stables, garages, conservatories and verandas may be converted into control breeding pens by thorough cleaning, redecoration and installation of wire pens. The breeder's requirements will determine the size and amount of pens. These pens ought to be about 6½ feet high by not less than 3 feet wide. The aviary should have a wire top to facilitate the catching of birds. Always bear in mind the dangers of limited space which can adversely affect breeding.

Certain buildings may be converted into flighted aviaries by adding a flight onto one side. Breeders often like to demonstrate their creativity by making these adapted flights as attractive as possible. Flowering plants, hedges and other assorted evergreens can give the birds protection from wind as well as beautifying an outdoor aviary setting.

Cockatiels do reproduce in cages with a reasonable amount of freedom. The breeder does have complete control over his birds by using breeding cages. The birds should only be housed in such cages for the duration of the breeding period; at other times they should have the freedom of pens or flights. If the birds are kept in cages all the time, they tend to deteriorate in general quality and in breeding potential. The cages for a single breeding pair or for half a dozen birds should be approximately 4 feet long, by 2 feet wide and 3 feet high.

Nest boxes can be hung on the side walls of cages to maximize internal space. The inspection of nests will be easier and during non-breeding periods the side entrance holes can be covered with hinged flaps. If bird room space is extremely limited, nest boxes can be hung onto wire fronts, but whenever possible sides should be used even if it means having one less tier of cages. The perches should be arranged as far apart as convenient but with enough space so the tails of the birds and flights do not rub against the sides. Nest boxes of the same type can be used for cages, pens, and aviaries.

The number of cockatiels kept as single family household pets has grown considerably in the past few years as people discover their charm. These birds are quite content living in the usual round or square all-wire parrot cages or in all wire-fronted cages. Cockatiels as pets should be taken into a household as soon as they can feed on their own which is approximately seven to eight weeks after hatching. Like all birds, each cockatiel differs in temperament; some are naturally tame and friendly, while others require coaxing

1

2

3

4

1. An average cockatiel nest contains five eggs. 2. A three-day-old (left) and a day-old baby cockatiel. The egg tooth is apparent at the tip of the upper mandible. 3. At the age of thirty-two days, the young cockatiel is ready to leave the nest. 4. A beautiful young bird, only hours out of the nest.

and patience. There are only a few birds that are not steady enough to tame. If after a reasonable amount of time the bird is found to be untrainable, it can be returned to an aviary for a replacement.

The best time to obtain a bird for training is during the spring and summer months. At this time the most suitable young birds are for sale. It is best to take a new bird home early in the day so it can have the maximum amount of time to settle down in its new quarters before nightfall. During the first few hours the bird should be left quietly on its own so it can explore and adjust to its new cage without disturbance. The bird will usually settle down after a few days. The owner can then teach his pet to talk; its name is usually the easiest to learn, and then short, simple, uncomplicated sentences. Once a bird is finger tamed it can be let loose in a room and taught to perform simple toy tricks. Generally, cock birds are the easiest to train as talking pets, but naturally a number of hens fulfill the requirements also. They can be taught to talk by using the same methods that are used in training parrots and parakeets. The word or short phrase is repeated to it as often as possible. Say the word first thing in the morning and the last thing at night. It will not be long before your bird will surprise you by repeating after you.

Cockatiels are often recommended as pets because they are easy to feed and are not unreasonably expensive. They are perfect for both young people and adults.

1. In a bird room or inside aviary, a fairly large cage is necessary to allow the birds sufficient room to exercise. 2. Wire mesh indoor breeding quarters for cockatiels; note the nest boxes attached to the cage sides.

1

2

1. Cockatiels that are
reared by hand often
remain very tame
even after several
years of aviary life. 2.
By preening itself the
bird shows the great
maneuverability of
the head. 3. Pied or
harlequin cockatiels
are very variable. The
desired symmetrical
pattern is rarely pro-
duced and transmit-
ted.

Feeding is never a problem with healthy cockatiels. It is best not to buy large quantities of seeds at one time, particularly in areas of high humidity. The seed should be stored in moisture-proof containers, especially if stored in a garage or outdoor feed shed.

Feeding and Foods

Cockatiels thrive and breed well on a simply prepared diet of seeds. The main seed mixture consists of mixed millets, bulk canary seeds, oats, mixed sunflower seeds, some hemp, and panicum millet. Both young and old birds are partial to ears of small millet seeds known as millet sprays. Young birds that have just left their nests will learn to feed themselves more quickly if they eat millet sprays. These sprays are also helpful in training cockatiels for exhibition purposes. Some breeders soak the millet sprays in cold water for twenty-four hours at breeding times; this practice, however, can stimulate the growth of molds. The breeder has his choice of the soaked or dry varieties.

Cockatiels must be given a regular supply of various fresh green foods if they are to maintain a fit, healthy and vigorous condition throughout the year. These birds eat foods such as chickweed, seeding grasses, spinach, lettuce, cabbage hearts, brussel sprouts, sowthistles, watercress, shepherds purse, chicory and slices of apples and carrots. All the green food should be given fresh daily and obtained from known clean sources. Sprouted seeds are also a good source of valuable food nutrients and are relished by parent birds when raising young. However, seeds should not be allowed to soak in water but just kept moist and in contact with air. When immersed in water the desired food nutrients leak out and reduce the value of this food. When the tiny sprouts are visible, they are ready for feeding. One can also prepare seedlings especially grown in a tray or pan. Small seeds are sprinkled in a pan with about one to two inches of moist clean soil and the seeds allowed to sprout and develop into small seedlings. To conserve moisture it can be covered with a plastic sheet. The whole tray or pan is then offered to the birds who will devour the seedlings, leaves, roots and all, including some of the soil. Uneaten food should be removed before it becomes stale or moldy.

Ample supplies of grits, cuttlefish bone, and mineral block are important to good health and perfect feathers. Additional mineral elements can be found in crushed dried domestic hen's eggshells, chalk, river and sea sand, and old mortar rubble.

Individual breeders have diverse ideas as to the best seed mixture for birds. There are, however, certain guide lines to follow. A mixture should not contain less than 40% of canary seed; added to this should be some 25% of mixed sunflower seeds coupled with a 35% mixture containing mixed millet, clipped oats, and a small quantity of hemp seed. Hemp, like sunflower seed, contains a high oil content and must be given in limited quantities which may be slightly increased during the cold winter months.

There are two major practices in giving seeds to cockatiels and other similar parrot-like birds. One technique favors all the seeds being mixed together in one dish, while the other approves of giving canary, sunflower and the other mixed seeds in 3 separate dishes or "cafeteria" style. Both methods are appropriate. A small problem can arise if an odd bird gets hooked on a particular type of seed in the separate method. This can make a bird too fat which is not desirable.

Soft food greatly helps cockatiels during breeding and molting periods. This food can take the form of a 50:50 mixture consisting of egg or raising food (as used for canaries) and a good insectivorous food. If the birds do not like this ratio, the owner may juggle the proportions until a happy balance is found. Occasionally a variation may be used. Whole meal bread moistened with plain water, boiled milk, honey water, or glucose and water can be offered. All uneaten soft food should be removed from cages, pens, or aviaries at the end of each day to prevent the birds from eating possible stale or sour food. Single pet cockatiels also benefit from the above mentioned food.

Most cockatiels like to take baths. Facilities are often provided for the bird's pleasure. Large, flat, shallow dishes, especially those made of earthenware, are best suited for this purpose and should be an addition to the bird's normal drinking vessel. If it is not possible to have a bathing dish in the pet cage, then a fine bird spray will do the job. When the bird becomes really tame it can bathe in the kitchen sink or in a bathroom under a slow dripping cold water tap.

Water used for drinking purposes can be placed in vessels similar to those used for seed feeding. Clip-on containers, which are better utilized in pens and cages, and water fountains (recommended for aviaries) also make good water vessels. These containers should all be placed clear of perches and away from seed and grit pots.

Mixed grits ought to be given in flat dishes and separated

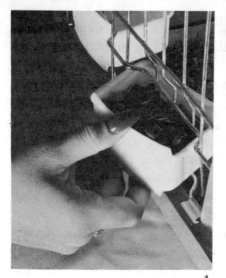

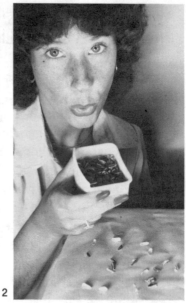

from other mineral elements such as chalk, old mortar rubble, and crushed dried domestic hen's eggshells. These latter materials should be placed in separate dishes. Pieces of cuttlefish bone and mineral blocks should be firmly fixed so birds may easily gnaw at them. If they are not attached they will be dropped, pulled about, and consequently soiled.

1. Some sunflower seed is needed, but don't overdo it! Sunflower seed contains a high oil content and must therefore be given in limited quantities which may be slightly increased during the cold winter months. 2. Cockatiels have a hard beak which enables them to crack the outer skin (or husk) of seeds; these husks have to be blown away daily. 3. When selecting your bird's staple diet, make sure that you also purchase a food to be used as an occasional treat. 4. Well stocked pet shops carry a wide enough range of staple and treat foods to cover all of your cockatiel's nutritional requirements.

In captivity, particularly in mild climates, it is not unusual to raise two broods per year; even more is possible, although not recommended. The entire breeding cycle takes about 2½ months from the time the eggs are laid until the chicks are weaned. *Below:* Breeding pairs separated from each other by wire mesh.

Breeding

Cockatiels are universally considered one of the most free-breeding members of the parrot-like species. Their breeding management is similar to that of the budgerigar. The quantity of cockatiels being produced has unquestionably led to the many color mutations that has further increased the bird's culture.

If strains are to be viable, only fully matured birds of the best quality can be bred. Most cockatiels will attempt to breed before they are twelve months old, but to use immature birds can be a disaster at a later date. The best breeding results are achieved by using birds older than eighteen to twenty-four months old. These mature birds can be expected to produce healthy young for four or five seasons.

Closely related birds should not be bred together; inbreeding of stock leads to the production of inferior young. Only fully experienced breeders who have special knowledge of inbreeding and have a definite objective in view should be allowed to inbreed their birds. Indiscriminate breeding from closely related stock invariably leads to poor quality birds (some with abnormalities) being produced, along with a sharp decline in the health, substance and breeding potential of the stud.

The initial stock of birds should be unrelated and procured from widely separate breeding studs. If these birds are not ringed with either closed or split rings the new owner should ring them on receipt of the birds. Metal and celluloid split rings can also be used for this purpose. Closed metal rings are permanent; they identify the birds and allow the breeder to make and keep positive breeding records. They are also available with etched coded numbers. When stock birds are first received their ring number or ring color should be entered in a register along with any other particulars. Within several seasons the owner will have a complete history of the stock inscribed in the register. This method will enable the breeder to mate the stock without any problems caused by close inbreeding or by split character mistakes that are carried by the birds.

A positive and permanent identification can be made of the young cockatiels by having them ringed with numbered and year-dated closed metal rings when they are between six and ten days old. The same method of ringing as used for budgerigars can be used in cockatiels too. The chick being ringed is held in the hand with one leg between the thumb and the first finger. The three longest toes are brought together as the ring is slipped along the shank and over the small hind toe. The small toe is then pulled free of the ring with the aid of a toothpick, matchstick or similar object. The chick may squeak quite loudly during this procedure, but it is not from being hurt—it is due to its indignity at being handled. Nests of chicks can be identified on sight by attaching colored celluloid rings with the closed rings. These colored rings allow the breeder to pick out special birds in the flights without having to catch and handle them.

The majority of healthy, fully mature cockatiels are ready to begin breeding in the spring around the beginning of March. The weather is very amenable; the days are growing longer and warmer, and the supply of numerous fresh green foods is becoming easier to obtain. Many breeders prefer to leave their mated pairs together all the time, while other owners opt to split up the pairs at the end of each breeding season. When the pairs are separated the sexes are kept apart in flights until they are needed for the next breeding season. This is the practice followed by most budgerigar breeders. Both these methods work well depending upon the available accommodations. It is up to the breeder to decide what he thinks will be most practical and effective for his stock.

Many experts favor the pairs being split apart with the sexes separate to achieve the best results from color breeding. This method not only allows the breeder to maintain strict control over the birds, but it also prevents the possibility of unwanted chance cross pairing. In addition, an advanced breeder may want to conduct experimental pairing with his stock; it is very important that there be no doubt with respect to the parentage of the bird used.

Prior to the actual breeding season prospective pairings should be made on paper with each bird's pedigree checked against the stock register. This technique will ensure that the breeder chooses the right crosses to give the most satisfactory results and that closely related birds are not mated together. The pedigrees of all breeding pairs used in color matching must be checked annually. This procedure is very important and includes all normals or mutations.

If mated pairs have been left together in aviaries, pens or

cages during the year, the breeder can position nest boxes when he feels his birds are fully fit and ready for breeding. Pairs that are freshly mated should be given five to seven days to become properly acquainted before giving them nest boxes. In this time they can settle down, mate, and get in the right mood for successful reproduction.

It is usual for clutches of eggs to start appearing in the nest boxes fifteen to twenty days after fully fit, ready-to-breed adult matched pairs are brought together. The number of eggs per clutch can range from three to ten; most of the large clutches are produced by older mature hens. The eggs are glossy white, oval in shape, and vary from 26 to 28 mm by 19 to 21 mm in size. Cockatiels, like budgerigars, lay their eggs on alternate days. This means there will be a few days difference between hatching of the first and last chicks of a nest. Actually, the length of time is governed by whether or not the parents start to sit from the first or subsequent eggs. Each egg has an incubation period of twenty-one days. The parents will take equal care of the young regardless of their age. It is extremely rare for the smallest chicks in a nest come to any harm.

Whether an egg is fertile or not is easily tested by candling. A fertile egg when seen through a strong source of light (lighted candle, flashlight, sunlight) shows traces of the developing embryo surrounded by a network of blood capillaries. Infertile eggs are clear and they should be removed from the nest.

Newly hatched cockatiel chicks covered with long, yellowish, silky down are usually considered ugly and it is not until other feathers develop that they begin to look like birds. Both members of breeding pairs will take their turn at incubating the eggs. Cock birds sit during the day, while their partners sit at night. Both sexes equally share the duty of feeding the young, but cock birds do not seem to feed their mates while young are in the nest. Males appear to think feeding the hens is a waste of time, since the female then passes the food on to the chicks, so they may just as well feed the young directly. Cockatiels do not mind if a breeder inspects the nest boxes as long as this is not done too frequently. It is rare to find a pair deserting their young as a protest against the nest interference.

There are numerous varieties of nest boxes that can be used for cockatiels. The most popular among breeders are the upright and flat types. The upright nest box is approximately 15 inches deep, 10 inches wide and long, with a 2½ inch square or round entrance hole near the top. Just below this entrance a perch is fixed and a hinged door is on the top for easy inspection. The dimensions of the flat type are 10 inches deep, by 10 inches wide, and 15 inches long with the entrance hole and perch at one side and the inspection door on the top. These measurements can be somewhat varied if it suits the breeder's particular requirements. It is convenient to have loose, concave bottoms covered with either a good layer of peat, coarse pine saw dust, soft wood shavings (or chips), or a mixture of these materials. These prevent the eggs from rolling. The majority of nesting hen birds seem to prefer a mixture of materials.

Young cockatiels are fully feathered and ready to leave their nest boxes when they are approximately five weeks old. Due to differences in hatching times, several days will elapse before an entire nest has flown. The young birds are fed by their parents for a week or ten days after they have left the nest. The owner should not move the birds from the breeding quarter until he is certain that the young can adequately fend for themselves. The chicks must have access to plenty of the usual seed, millet sprays, grits and various fresh green food both before and after they are taken from their parents.

When needed, some breeders favor the practice of fostering eggs and chicks. The eggs may have been abandoned; if fertile, they are transfered to other nests with eggs of about the same age. This is the one instance when having more

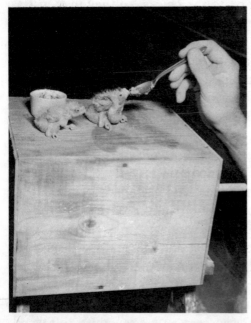

1. Handfeeding is one of the greatest aids to the cockatiel owner in taming the bird. Once the cockatiel's trust is won, the job is half over. 2. With its wings held away from the body, the chick takes the food from the male. 3. A scooped-out dish is not always necessary, for many times the eggs are laid on the bare floor if the nest box is large enough.

than one pair of birds mate at about the same time is desirable. However, be sure that the eggs are identified and the ensuing chicks banded as early as possible. Parents may also stop feeding or start feather picking one or more chicks. The alternatives are either to hand-feed or foster these young. Hand-feeding is possible, but it is tedious, time consuming and impractical when one has many birds to care for. The chick is placed in a nest with chicks of about the same age; foster parents may refuse a much younger chick and it may be left to perish.

3

Most cockatiels that are taken into households as pets are of normal gray type, although all colors are equal in their potential as tame (and often talking) pets. It is mainly because of their cost that examples of the newer mutations are not often trained as pets.

The Normal Gray Cockatiel

In this and the following sections color descriptions will be given of the major types of cocks and hens. These detailed descriptions of areas of color will enable readers to visualize the birds more clearly as they look at the illustrations that appear within this book. As mentioned previously, there were no actual subspecies recorded among the wild flocks; there are, however, some slight tone differences in birds taken from widely separated habitats. These slight differences can also be seen in various domesticated strains along with their mutant colors.

Cock: The general overall color of the body comprises various shades of gray: the deepest tone is on the underside of the long pointed tail, and the palest shade of gray is found along the two center feathers. The front of the head, cheeks and throat are lemon yellow, and the outward curving crest (approximately 1-1¼ inches long) is a mixture of yellow and gray. The sides of the head are white with large red-orange patches. There is a broad white bar on each wing tinted very pale yellow; this bar runs from the shoulders to the secondary wing coverts. Each wing has a broad white bar tinted with very light yellow extending from the "elbow" across the wing coverts. The eyes are brown, while the beak, feet, and legs are gray of various intensities. Total length including the tail is approximately 13 inches.

Hen: The general body color is very much like the cock's except that the wing bars and eye patches are less pure in color. The ear patches are not as extensive in the female, and the crown lacks white. The yellow areas are only very faintly tinted. In fact, the yellow areas tend to be more grayish in hue. The hen's thighs are barred with pale yellow and the underside of her tail is striped and dappled with gray and yellow; the overall gray coloring is duller than on the cock and often has a faint brownish cast on it. A very mature hen's general color deepens quite considerably and it becomes difficult to distinguish them from first-year cocks. Hens are about 11-12 inches in total length.

Immature Birds: These are paler editions of the hen. They do not get yellow on their facial area until they are approximately six months old, and it is not until several months later that they assume full adult coloring. Feathered cockatiel nestlings are difficult to sex. Those with the brightest colors usually turn out to be cocks, but this color test is not always true; do not take it as a sure guide.

Domesticated cockatiels derived from wild-type birds are

more substantially built than the newer mutant colors and for this reason are extensively used for outcrossing. There are many first-class strains of pure normals from which exhibition birds are derived. Overall substance and general depth of color can be improved by carefully selecting parent birds—in fact, this is the only way a color strain may be developed with the quality maintained.

Most household pet cockatiels are of the normal gray type. All colors are equal in taming and talking potential, but new mutations do cost more; this aspect might have an influence on the color choice of pets.

Pairs of normal grays will produce only gray colored offspring, except in cases of chance mutations or of mutant colors being carried unknown to the breeder. If a lot of cross-pairing does take place for the sake of the stock improvement, then second and third generation birds will often be disposed of as normals.

The albino is a mutation that quickly caught the imagination of many breeders of parrot-like birds because of the drastic color differences between it and the normal gray.

The Albino Cockatiel

The color differences between this mutation and the normal gray quickly caught the imagination of many breeders of parrot-like birds. Albino cockatiels are white ground birds like the gray or blue series in budgerigars, and therefore possess red-orange ear patches and varying amounts of yellow suffusion on their bodies. Genetically, albino character removes all dark coloring from a bird's plumage, but does not affect the yellow or red-orange color; these light and dark hues are produced by entirely different pigments. This fact causes many breeders to call these birds lutinos or yellows, especially those albinos with an extra

extra amount of yellow suffusion. Yellowness may be increased in depth and extent by careful selection of the breeding stock.

Cock: Pure white is found in the general areas that are gray in the normal cockatiel. The throat, part of the cheeks, and front of the head are lemon yellow. The crest is a mixture of yellow and white, and the ear patches are the normal shade of red-orange. The wings have areas of yellow. There is a yellow cast or tinge on the tail. The eyes are red, the beak is a yellow horn color, and the feet and legs are flesh pink.

Hen: A yellow cast on the thighs and under the tail differentiates the general coloring between the two sexes.

Immature birds: These young show less yellowing than adults and are difficult to sex until they are fully matured. Their eyes are a lighter but brighter shade of red than those of an adult. Even some fully adult albinos are difficult to sex and only by careful observation of their behavior towards one another can they be sexed.

The character that causes albino coloring is sex-linked in the manner of inheritance. By making certain pairings, the breeder can use sex-linked mutations to control the sex of a color. This knowledge can be very useful when young cock birds are needed to train as tame talking pets. The following rules of albino inheritance will show the breeder what matings can be made so young cocks can be identifiable at hatching.

1) Albino cock x albino hen gives 100% albino cocks and hens. 2) Albino cock x normal gray hen gives 50% normal gray/albino cocks, 50% albino hens. 3) Albino hen x normal gray cock gives 50% normal gray/albino cocks, 50% normal gray hens. 4) Albino hen x normal gray/albino cock gives 25% albino cocks, 25% albino hens, 25% normal gray albino cocks, 25% normal gray hens. 5) Normal gray/albino cock x normal gray hen gives 25% normal gray cocks, 25%

normal gray hens, 25% normal gray albino cocks, 25% albino hens.

Presently, the majority of albinos in existence are the albino form of the normal gray. It is possible, though, to have an albino form of all the other mutations both in their pure and "split" form, all of which look alike. Because of this, albino parents carrying various color characters may have young of different colors in their nests. The breeder will be able to discover the reason why other colors have appeared if he keeps good and accurate records. An undesirable character, baldness, has appeared in albino cockatiels and breeders are trying very hard to eliminate this apparently dominant trait from their stock.

Once you become seriously interested in breeding color varieties of the cockatiel you have to study the mechanics of inheritance, amply covered in some of the larger specialized cockatiel books available.

The pied mutation is *not* sex-linked. Before a pied can be produced, both its parents must carry the factor, and this mode of inheritance is more common than sex linkage.

The Pied Cockatiel

Breeders have tried for many years to produce the pied (also known as variegated) cockatiel. Birds were being bred with extra odd white feathers in their plumage, but these mismarked specimens were not pied cockatiels. It was not until a mutation appeared that the pied strain was finally established. The character that gives the broken color appearance is recessive and can be carried by other colors, both by cock and hen in "split" form.

Cock: These birds are similar in color to the normal gray and have patches of different sizes that interrupt the dark color. These clear, irregularly shaped patches are white and yellow tinted with white. Individual birds have assorted clear areas; some specimens possess small patches, while others are extensively marked. Most of the birds seem to have a 50:50 color arrangement. The beak and eyes are like those of a normal gray, but the feet and legs can be gray, fleshy pink, or a mixture of both.

Hen: The female is similar to the normal gray and like the cock has white and yellow tinted with white areas that break the basic color of the plumage.

Immature Birds: The young are merely paler versions of the hen. They do not have clearly defined lines of demarcation in their broken areas.

When a pied normal gray cock or hen is paired to a normal gray all the young produced will be normal gray in color, but genetically they will be different. Birds resulting from this crossing of these two colors are known as normal gray/pied, and when given suitable mates they can produce actual pied young. The pied character is inherited in the usual recessive manner as shown in the table below:

1) Pied normal gray x normal gray gives 100% normal gray/pied cocks and hens. 2) Pied normal gray x normal gray pieds gives 50% pied normal gray cocks and hens. 3) Normal gray/pied x normal gray/pied gives 25% normal gray cocks and hens, 50% normal gray/pied cocks and hens, 25% pied normal gray cocks and hens. 4) Normal gray/pied x normal gray gives 50% normal gray cocks and hens, 50% normal gray/pied cocks and hens. 5) Pied normal gray x pied normal gray gives 100% pied normal gray cocks and hens.

Since there is no sex-linkage involved, it is immaterial as to which member of a pair is the pied normal gray or the "split." Notice that in crossings 3 and 4 two genetical types

This is a male opaline at first molt; the opaline or pearled pattern is rapidly being replaced by solid gray plumage.

are produced which have no visual difference; this can only be discovered by test pairing.

It is essential that normal gray/pieds be used regularly in pairings if a stud of the pied normal gray is to be improved and maintained. The best results are obtained when the "split" birds are from crossing normal gray to pied normal gray. This rule applies to all color matings where "split" birds are used. The birds from such crosses are known as first cross "splits."

Bear in mind that it is possible to produce actual clear white (but non-albino) birds by selective breeding. Cockatiels with the largest clear areas can be bred together to produce young with a greater expanse of light feathers. After generations of this selective pairing it is possible that the desired objective of clear white birds may be reached. Such whites have dark eyes.

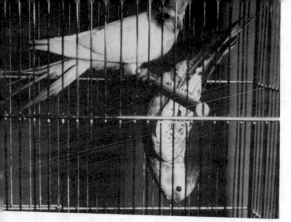

The pearled cockatiel first occurred in West Germany in 1967 or perhaps 1968. Rumor has it that the same mutation was found in Belgian birds the year after its appearance in German birds. *Right:* albino and pearled; *below:* pearled, albino, and normal gray cockatiels.

The Pearled Cockatiel

The pearled mutation is an unexpected happening. Like the opaline in the budgerigar family, the originally named pearled has a change of feather pattern—not a change of color.

Pearled cockatiels are fairly recent arrivals so they are relatively limited in number and tend to be somewhat expensive. Several birds have appeared at exhibitions where they have been greatly admired, and more than ever, there is an increasing demand for this novel variety.

This bird's inheritance is sex-linked like the albino. The expectations for pearled mating can be worked out by adapting those obtained for albino matings. There can be pearled forms of other mutations; so far pied pearled and fawn pearled have been produced by enthusiastic breeders.

Cock: These birds are somewhat like the normal gray, but vary in wing pattern. Two shades of gray coloring occupy large areas of wing feathers which create a definite attractive pattern combination. The pattern on the wings is variable in its markings and in the sex-linked nature of its inheritance. The orange-red color of the ear patches and the yellow suffusion on certain areas are not as intense as on the normal gray. The eyes are clear brown and the beak is gray. The feet and legs are in different tones of gray; sometimes they even have a pinkish undertone.

Hen: The female's general body color is like the cock with a few exceptions: her ear patches are not as extensive, nor are they as rich as the male's, and her wing bars are less pure in color. The white on the crown is absent, and the yellow areas are a bit fainter than the cock. Her thighs are barred with pale yellow and the underside of the tail is striped and dappled with clear gray and yellow.

Immature Birds: These young are paler than the adults. Their pattern markings are less clear and more variable in their distribution.

Breeders have found that the pearled character of the plumage persists in the females but fades in the males after the first molt or if not, later in the second year. So banding of the birds is quite important, for the character may not be recognized visually.

This young female cockatiel is fully mature sexually. Cockatiels generally are able to breed by the time they are about half a year old, but their first breeding attempts are not always successful.

Subdued in over-all coloration, the fawn cockatiel is a comparatively recent development. Fawn birds are derived from mutations in birds, such as the albino shown below, having a white ground color.

Rarer Color Varieties

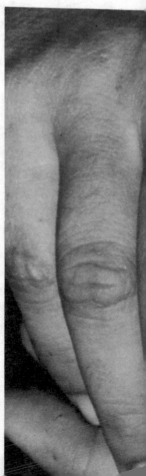

THE FAWN (CINNAMON) COCKATIEL

With the domestication of most species of birds, sooner or later there will appear a cinnamon form in yellow ground birds and a fawn form in white ground. Fawns (cinnamon) were reported to have been bred a considerable time ago, but it was not until recently that details and live specimens became available. It was not recorded when these mutations first appeared, but examples have turned up in Australia, America and Europe during the last twenty-five years. In Europe this mutation is called cinnamon and Isabelle. These birds ought to be termed "fawn" for they are white ground birds just like the

canaries and zebra finches where a white ground bird is involved. The actual color of fawn cockatiels is more of a gray-brown than a cinnamon-brown shade commonly associated with other domestic birds.

Cocks: The general overall body color is a variety of grayish brown hues. The deepest tone is on the underside of the long pointed tail, while the palest shade is found with the two central feathers. The front of the head, cheeks and throat are lemon yellow, and the crest is a mixture of yellow and grayish brown. The sides of the crown are white. The large ear patches are red-orange. Each wing has a broad white bar tinted pale yellow that runs from the elbow to the secondary wing coverts. The eyes are brown, the beak is grayish horn in color, and the feet and legs are pinkish.

Hens: The female is very much like the male in general body color, except her ear patches are not as extensive nor as rich in color. The wing bars are also less pure in color. The white is absent from the crown and the yellow areas are only faintly tinted and tend to be more grayish brown. The thighs are barred with yellow, while the underside of the tail is striped and spotted with grayish brown and yellow. Like the normal gray, the color deepens with age in very mature hens, and it becomes difficult to distinguish them from the first year cocks.

Immature Birds: These young are paler editions of the hen. They do not get yellow on their facial area until they are several months old and it is not until they are in their eighth to tenth month that they assume full adult coloring.

All fawn (cinnamon) varieties have pinkish flesh color eyes when they are first hatched. This characteristic sharply contrasts with the similar black-eyed normal grays. This trait, though, does enable a breeder to immediately identify fawns that were produced by cross-pairings while they are still in the nest.

Fawn cockatiels do offer plenty of scope for color improvement as their general overall color may be developed into a brown shade. This can be done by selecting the best colored fawns and mating them with pale normals, and then mating the resulting birds together. After a few seasons of careful selection, the color of fawns should be improved. The objective is to eliminate all gray overtones.

THE DILUTE COCKATIEL

Most breeds of domesticated birds will eventually produce a dilute mutation where the color is seen in varying degrees less than its full strength. These birds are paler and brighter than normal grays and are often called dilute or silver cockatiels. Since this mutation is relatively new, information about these birds is somewhat scant. The dilute mutation is now considered a recessive breeding type (recessive is the more popular notion). It is possible that these birds have been developed by selective pairings of pale normal grays over a period of time. Dilute birds are really paler and brighter gray than the normal gray and deserve to be called silver. If this coloration is indeed man-made, then it demonstrates what can be done with perseverance and care in breeding aviaries. As sufficient stock becomes available, more breeding experiments will be engaged and soon their status will be completely answered.

Cock: The dilute has the characteristic lemon yellow on its cheeks, throat, and front of head. Its general overall body color is different shades of silver-gray. Again, the deepest tones are found along the underside of the long pointed tail, and the palest color is located within the two central feathers. The large ear patches are red-orange, and the sides of the crown are white. The dilute has reddish-brown eyes, a grayish beak, and pinkish legs and feet. Each wing has a broad white bar with pale yellow running its course from the elbow to the secondary wing coverts.

Hen: Its general body color is similar to the cock, but the ear patches are not as large or as bright. The wing bars are

1. Indoors or outdoors, the cockatiel is a lovely bird, but its sedate beauty can best be appreciated in a natural outdoor setting. 2. Seed and water containers should be made of a non-porous, easy-to-clean material. 3. The proudly erect carriage of a healthy cockatiel of any color variety, coupled with the magnificent crest, creates great visual appeal.

2

3

1. The design of many cages is extremely decorative; cages are often painted in neutral colors to make the birds even more pleasing to the eye. There is no reason to condemn a cage of this sort out of hand, but few will disagree with the statement that this is a cage with very definite limitations. 2. A female (right) and a male cockatiel (left). Note the conspicuous lighter-colored area on the head of the male. 3. Pesticidal agents useful in eliminating bird parasites are available in many different forms; here an aerosol is being used.

1

2

less pure in color, the underside of the tail is striped and dappled with yellow and silver-gray, and the thighs are barred with yellow. The hen lacks white on her crown and has faintly tinted yellow areas that are actually more silver-gray than the cock.

Immature birds: Like other cockatiels, these are the paler edition of the hen.

Since the dilute form is recessive, it will be inherited in the same manner as the pied character.

Cockatiel breeding has greatly increased and soon there should be additional developed color varieties. As each new mutation appears, the number of possible composite types increases; this adds excitement to the breeding and exhibiting of cockatiels.

3

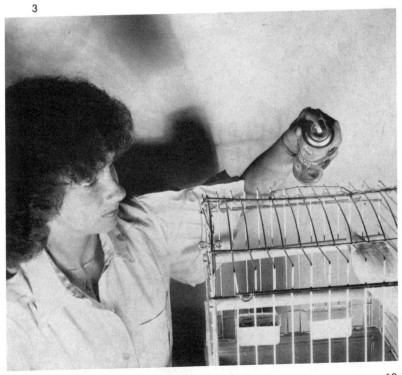

1. Judging by color pattern alone, this pearled cockatiel could be either a female or immature male, but it could not be a fully adult male; a fully adult male would have molted its pearled plumage and become a basically gray bird. 2. A very nice pair of lutinos. 3. During emergencies a cockatiel that is showing signs of illness or fighting with its cage mates can be housed temporarily until the proper accommodation is found or established.

3

COMPOSITE COLOR VARIETIES

It is possible through a series of matings to produce a cockatiel that shows the characters of two or more mutations. The only existing mutation that does not visually combine with others is the albino, and this is due to its overall loss of dark coloring. The pied can be bred in fawn (Note: fawn here is always understood to be connected with cinnamon), pearled, and dilute forms. It is also possible to have pied fawn pearled, pied fawn dilute, and pied pearled dilute cockatiels. The pearled can be had in pearled fawn, pearled dilute, and pearled fawn dilute.

It takes at least two seasons to produce a combination of the pied character because it is recessive. After this amount of time production is relatively simple. The pied pearled can be bred by crossing a pearled cock with a normal pied gray hen. This cross produces normal gray/pearled cocks and normal gray/pied hens. The next season normal gray/pied cocks can be paired to normal gray pied hens and this will give 25% pied pearled gray hens among their young. This procedure will give the breeder the correct stock for the following season if he wishes to produce both cocks and hens of the pied pearled gray form.

The pied fawn can be bred similarly to the pied pearled since the fawn character is also sex-linked. The first step in this project involves pairing a fawn cock to a pied hen—this cross gives normal gray/pied fawn cocks and normal gray/pied hens. When these young cocks are paired back to normal pied hens they give 25% of the desired pied fawn hens. In the following year cocks of this color can be bred by pairing the pied fawn hens to the "split" cocks.

Birds that have three color characters (pied, fawn and pearled) can be raised from a number of different crosses

1. Cover the cage in the evening so the bird can go to sleep. 2. Make sure that you play with and inspect your cockatiel regularly.

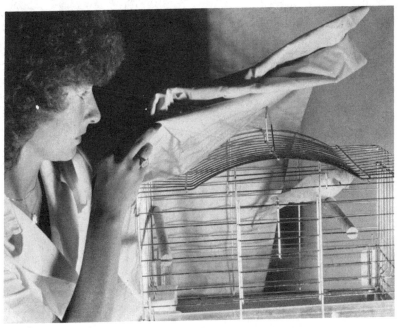

1   2

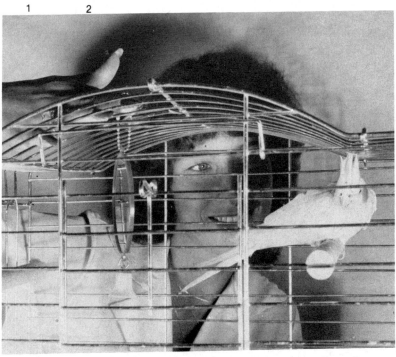

The normal gray cockatiel is still, despite the in-
troduction of new color varieties, the most popular
and inexpensive type of cockatiel. 1. A young male
normal gray coming into color. 2. A fully adult male
normal gray.

2

1

2

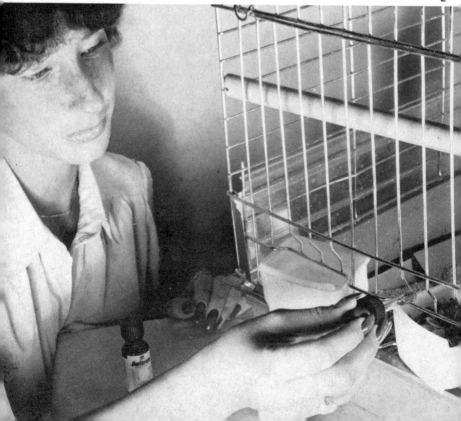

where the birds have the necessary characters either visually or in "split" form. Once pied fawn cocks have been bred they can then be mated to pied pearled hens which will produce normal pied/fawn pearled cocks and pied fawn hens. In turn, the normal pied/fawn pearled cocks can be mated to either pied pearled or pied fawn hens. From either of these matings will come some pied pearled fawn hens together with a number of other useful breeding birds.

The dilute (silver) character can be used to create further color varieties such as dilute (silver) pearled, dilute (fawn) dilute (silver) pied, dilute (silver) pearled fawn, dilute (silver) pied fawn, dilute (silver) pied pearled, and dilute (silver) pied pearled fawn. By including the dilute (silver) character in composite forms the resulting birds are a softer shade of color which makes them distinct from the ordinary gray shade. A paler and somewhat altered tone of color of bird is produced when the fawn character is introduced. Due to the basic color of cockatiels, the present mutant colors will be a little paler but still discernible from the normal gray. Since the number of mutations has been increasing, there can and will be a considerable amount of different colors and combinations of the cockatiel. It should be noted that many of the composite forms mentioned in this chapter have yet to be produced by the enterprising breeder.

1. Very few foods contain all the elements that are essential for correct feeding. Fortunately it is not necessary for the bird-fancier to sit down to calculate caloric intake and nutritional compounds, because in the case of birds correct feeding can usually be achieved simply by providing a wide variety of different foods. The wider this variety the greater the chance there is that all the essentials of correct feeding will have been covered. 2. Vitamin and mineral supplements that can be used to fortify the basic cockatiel diet in captivity are economical and easy to use.

Learning the proper way to show cockatiels is something which has to be acquired by experience. Beginners are well advised to join a bird club to obtain valuable pointers about successful bird exhibiting. The birds shown at right and below, for example, have faults that would place them at a disadvantage in show competition.

Exhibiting Cockatiels

The potential of cockatiels as exhibition birds is just now being explored. Until recently very few show-promoting societies had an actual separate class solely for cockatiels. At most shows cockatiels must be exhibited in mixed parakeet classes with new colors going in abnormally colored classes. Many breeders would probably exhibit more of their birds if they were given encouragement in the form of separate classes. Breeders can help this situation by voicing their requests when local shows are considering classifications.

Cockatiels are excellent show birds either as single or true pairs. They settle down quickly and become tame and amenable in a show cage. At present there are no standard show cages required for cockatiels, and consequently they are exhibited in various types of cages deemed suitable by their owners. Many of these cages have a lengthwise perch that enables the birds to sit with their breast or back to the judge. Other breeders prefer to follow the style of the standard budgerigar show cage.

The budgerigar style show cage is excellent for the all around appraisal of the bird's merits from an exhibition angle. A recommended size cage for a pair of cockatiels is 18 inches long, by 9 inches deep, and 16 inches high, with two centrally placed perches. Until a standard show cage is adopted cockatiels can be shown in any suitably sized cage. The cage should be clean and well painted.

To do well in a show a cockatiel must have a reasonable amount of show training beforehand. When selecting birds for show the relationship of the chosen birds is not important since this is not for breeding purposes. The selected pairs should each be put into a stock cage (that is larger than four feet) weeks before they are required for actual showing. An old show cage can be hung over the open door of the stock cage with green food or millet sprays in it to entice the birds inside. After a short time the birds will be accustomed to going in and out of the show cage. Then they can be shut in for short periods at the beginning, and gradually the time of confinement can be increased. It is surprising how quickly these pairs adapt to the change in accommodation, for they soon become quite at ease in their smaller cages. In addition, a show cockatiel must be trained not to be afraid of strangers looking at it from close range. The judge cannot really evaluate a bird that is constantly moving or if it is huddled in a corner of the cage. While the pairs are in the stock cages a regular spraying with a fine water spray is helpful in keeping their plumage in the clean, silky condition required for exhibition.

Whether the show pairs are normal grays or a new color, the principle of selection is the same in all cases. Each bird should be a good, well-colored example of its variety and have plenty of substance, unbroken and clean feathers, a clean beak, and no toes or nails missing.

Normal birds are judged according to uniformity and quality of the gray coloration. Ticking (random white feathers among the gray) is considered a flaw. With specimens of the pied variety the clear areas should match each other as near as possible; symmetry of piedness is a great consideration. 40% to 60% pied condition is adequate. It is also desirable to have more tail and flight feathers clear. With respect to the albino cockatiel, some breeders prefer to develop either a more white bird or a more yellow bird. The bald spot is undesirable in the white variety of cockatiel for showing; no splotching is allowed.

Only true pairs of the same color can be shown together so it is important to make well-balanced pairs. It is not advisable to exhibit any pair too frequently, especially if they are to be used later for breeding purposes.

2

1. Cuttlebone, either in powdered form or as the actual skeleton of the squid, should always be available. Cockatiels like cuttlebone, and apparently the calcium it contains is readily absorbed by them.

2. Lutinos or albinos are, by definition, sex-linked, which means that a male lutino must have had a lutino mother. But a lutino hen obtains her color wholly from her father. The color of her mother is immaterial. Therefore lutino hens can be bred from lutino males, but a male lutino must have a lutino or a split lutino father as well as a lutino mother.

— 1

Before you buy your cockatiel be sure to have all the necessary equipment; ask your local pet store for advice! Purchasing your bird and all of your equipment at a well-stocked pet shop or bird specialty store also can save you time and money.

The Cockatiel As A Household Pet

Each year more and more people are keeping cockatiels as household pets. These birds are easy to tame and finger train and are reasonable in cost when compared to other members of the parrot family. The cockatiel is not a prolific talker, but it can be taught to repeat a number of words and short sentences. Occasionally there will be a brilliant linguist among these birds.

To train as a tame talking pet, a young, fit, healthy cock bird should be selected and taken away from its parents as soon as it is seen feeding entirely on its own. Young hens can also be trained to become tame, talking, affectionate

1. The normal gray pied mutation. It is preferable that most tail and wing flights be clear, with the ideal being totally clear flight feathers. Symmetry of markings is more important than the percentage of piedness and will be the most important factor in judging the coloration aspects of this mutation. 2. A lutino mutation. Providing a standard name for this bird is difficult, as we have neither a true albino (there is still orange and yellow) nor a true lutino (solid yellow with orange cheek patch.) 3. Pair of adult cinnamons. Cinnamons originated in Belgium and are sex-linked. Their eyes are of a lighter brown than a normal's.

3

pets, but they are more temperamental and take longer to learn to talk than the cock. The prospective owner may have to rely on the breeder or pet shop for correct information on sexing the bird.

A cage should be obtained for the bird before it is even purchased. The cage can be a box type sized to fit in with the furnishings of a room, or it can be a more conventional round or square metal wire parrot-type cage. Ample food, water, and grit vessels must be positioned in the cage together with a piece of cuttlefish bone and a mineral nibble. The cage floor should be covered with sand or very fine gravel. The cage ought to be cleaned regularly.

It is best to get a bird early in the day so it has plenty of time to settle down in its new home well before roosting time. The bird should be allowed approximately eight to twelve days to become fully accustomed to its new surroundings before serious training is started. Some cockatiel owners, however, are of the opinion that a period of acclimation is not necessary and that young cockatiels can be tamed in a few hours. Sudden movements and loud noises must not be made around the cage. If the bird is to be kept in a room used often by the family a cover should then be placed over the cage so the bird will not be frightened by noise. The owner should speak to the new bird in a quiet, clear, even voice when giving fresh seed and water to the bird. Only one person in the household ought to train the cockatiel at first; this is done to prevent the bird from being confused by different voice tones and inflections.

When an owner feels that his bird has become thoroughly accustomed to its new home he can begin the first stages of training. The door should be opened and a piece of millet spray or green food should be offered slowly to the bird. Remember to hold the food steady as the bird nibbles at the offering. In most cases it does not take long before the bird is eating out of the owner's hands without showing signs of nervousness. The next step is to gradually ease a finger beneath the bird's feet so it can sit on a finger while eating food from the other hand. As soon as the bird is sitting fearlessly, it can be pulled slowly towards the open door, out into the room, and then back into the cage. Once a bird reaches such a stage of tameness it will usually let the owner gently stroke its chest and tickle the back of its head.

After a while the cage door can be left open to let the bird fly around the room and get some much needed exercise. Whenever the bird is out of its cage all doors and windows must be firmly closed and all solid fuel, gas or electric appliances not be in use. Cut flowers and potted plants ought to be removed from the room since they attract cockatiels (if the improper green plants are eaten they will have a bad effect upon the bird's digestion).

A pet cockatiel can be easily fed with a mixture of sunflower seed, canary seed, mixed millets, and a few clipped oats. Sometimes new owners like to ask the breeder or pet store owner what kind of seed mixture the bird has been eating and what type should be used. Most cockatiels are extremely fond of various green foods, and whenever possible a small quantity should be given to them daily.

Care and consideration in housing, feeding and general overall management of a cockatiel is important if the pet is to give its owner years of interesting and pleasurable companionship. There should not be any trouble healthwise if the bird was healthy when first obtained. If the bird does appear to be off color, or has very ruffled feathers, or loose droppings, do seek advice. Bird breeders can often be of help, but in many cases the pet owner should seek veterinary assistance.

Wing Clipping

An unclipped household pet bird should never be taken outdoors uncaged; the chance of its flying away is great and the possibility of retrieving an escaped bird is sometimes miniscule. If recapturing a bird is possible, some damage

2

1. Lutino is one of the most beautiful mutations on the market! Both sexes are alike and have dark red eyes, yellow head and crest, orange cheek patches and varying degrees of yellow on the rest of the body and flights. Baldness is a unique fault in lutino and seems to be a dominant factor in breeding. Sometimes the hen has a yellow wash on the thighs and under the tail. 2. Sexing gray or normal cockatiels is easy, as the female is much duller than the male, with the facial markings much reduced and the undersides of the tail feathers irregularly barred with yellow.

← 1

91

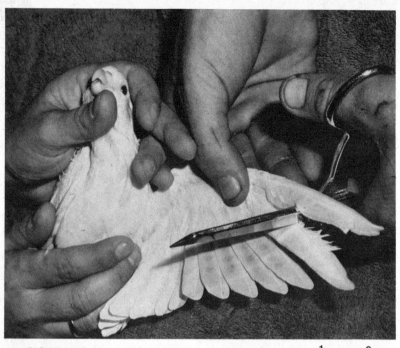

1   2

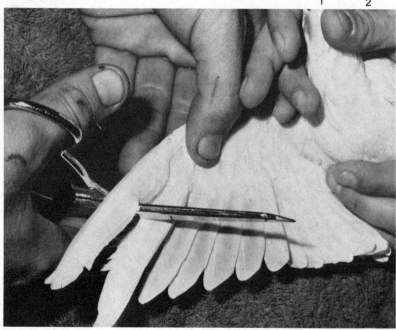

sometimes results from the process, such as loss of feathers, broken wing or leg. To ensure the safety of the bird several means have been devised to prevent its flying away other than actual confinement in a cage. Even in the confines of a closed room, unclipped birds can injure themselves flying straight into the wall or window or window glass pane. Birds kept in aviaries and flighted brooding pens do not need to be clipped, since they are fairly secure unless the keeper and his help are very careless and leave doors open.

Wing clipping is a painless and simple procedure. It will not cause pain or harm unless the skin or flesh is damaged. With the aid of another person who holds the bird around the body firmly and spreads the wing out, one person cuts some particular feathers off one or both wings. There are two suggested styles of clipping: in one method all the primaries (principal flight feathers) are cut from either the left or right wing; in the other method some secondaries and the primaries (except a few outer ones) of both wings are cut. In the second method the symmetrical appearance of the wings is preserved.

Instead of cutting the wing feathers some keepers prefer to pluck the primaries. They state that it is also a painless process. Flight can also be inhibited temporarily by simply taping the upper and undersides of flight feathers. The tape is removed when no longer needed.

With molting, new feathers replace the clipped or pluck-ed ones. If there is still need to restrict flight, the procedure is repeated before the bird is fully feathered and capable of flying again.

Wing-clipping is quick and easy. 1. One person holds the cockatiel securely while the other does the actual clipping. The bird must be held firmly but gently. 2. The holder carefully extends one wing, which then can be clipped of all the primary feathers except the outer two or three.